A Voice *for* The VOICE

For Pastors and Anyone Speaking on Behalf of the Lord

Michael C. Turner Sr.

A Voice for the VOICE
For Pastors and Anyone Speaking on Behalf of the Lord
Copyright © 2018 by Michael C. Turner Sr.

No part of this book may be reproduced, stored in a retrieval system, or transmitted in any form or by any means without expressed written permission of the author. Thank you for your support of the author's rights.

Scriptures are from the King James Version of the Holy Bible. Copyright © 1972 by Thomas Nelson Inc., Camden, New Jersey 08103.

Certain pronouns capitalized in Scripture that refer to the Father, Son and Holy Spirit is the author's choice as well as emphasis within Scripture quotations.

www.TheMiracleCenterFMBC.com

ISBN: 978-1-7324232-0-6
Library of Congress In Publication Data
Category: Self-Help / Motivational & Inspirational / Faith / Christian

Written by: Michael C. Turner Sr. | bishopturner55@gmail.com
Cover Design & Book Formatting: Eli Blyden | CrunchTime Graphics *for Publishing*
Formatting Assistant: Jahshua E. Blyden

Printed in the United States of America by: A&A Printing & Publishing

Dedication

*To my spirit-filled supportive wife,
Bishop Eunice Thomas Turner,
a mighty voice for The Voice.*

A Voice *for* The VOICE

Table of Contents

Dedication iii

Foreword vii

Introduction 1

CHAPTER ONE
The Voice Is Always Calling Other Voices 5

CHAPTER TWO
Who Me? God Is Calling You to Be a Voice 11

CHAPTER THREE
A Voice as a Contemporary Priest/Pastor 15

CHAPTER FOUR
A Voice as a Contemporary Prophet 21

CHAPTER FIVE
A Voice as a Present-Day Servant 27

CHAPTER SIX
Quotes from My Lips from The Voice 31

CHAPTER SEVEN
The Danger of Being a Voice 33

CHAPTER EIGHT
The Benefits of Being Obedient to The Voice 37

Conclusion 41

Acknowledgements 43

About the Author 45

Follow Bishop Michael C. Turner Sr. on Social Media.... 49

Foreword

It is indeed an honor to write the foreword for the book entitled, "*A Voice for the VOICE*" by Bishop Michael C. Turner, Sr. I had the privilege of meeting Bishop Turner through my friendship with his anointed and gifted wife, Bishop Eunice T. Turner, who is a prayer warrior. He is the Senior Pastor of The Miracle Center of Faith Missionary Baptist Church in Maryland. Bishop Turner participates in spiritual outreach and missionary work and serves as a Spiritual Shepherd to many local and international churches. He is also the founder and the Presiding Bishop of the International Evangelism College of Bishops which was established on December 15, 2016.

In the title of this book and throughout its pages, Bishop Turner encourages Bishops, Apostles, Pastors and anyone speaking on behalf of the Lord. This book is meant to inspire them in their role as voices. The book reminds them that they are not the Voice, but rather they are voices for the Voice. No doubt, it is a privilege to be chosen as a voice for the Voice. However, it is important that we do not inadvertently put our voices above that of the Absolute Voice. In this work, he also reminds humanity of the *Caller,* who summons others to speak on His behalf. Bishop Turner's passion is further revealed in affirming that the called-out-ones must stay focused on their divine assignment, which is to be a voice for the *Savior*, and not for *self.*

This book is a "must read" for anyone speaking on behalf of the Lord. The Holy Spirit anoints humble servants to bring about *His* plans and purposes. In this book, Bishop Turner has opened new windows of insight for anyone speaking on behalf of the Lord. It is a reminder of the necessity to stay within the boundaries of a voice and to succeed in the kingdom role. This work is not only insightful, but also revolutionary, as it creates a conscious awareness on the need to position oneself appropriately when speaking on behalf of the Lord. I recommend this book as a resource to many churches and ministries, for the insights it reveals in knowing that there is *only* one Voice - *The Absolute Voice.*

Reverend Henrietta C. Ekekezie
President & Founder,
Refreshing Glory Ministries Inc.
Maryland - USA

A Voice *for* The VOICE

*For Pastors and Anyone Speaking
on Behalf of the Lord*

A Voice *for* The VOICE

Introduction

In a dreamlike state, the Lord spoke to me as I was preparing to deliver a message to persons who were being ordained, licensed, and commissioned to various ministries, at a convention in Liberia. The Lord told me to use this theme, "A Voice for The Voice". He further instructed me to remind them that, "He is The Voice before voices". Now, this theme continued to linger in my spirit, and upon returning from Liberia for the fourth time in the last fourteen months, I was given the opportunity to preach the 30th Pastoral Anniversary of a pastor in Newport News, Virginia. Amazingly, this same Voice returned to me again saying, "Preach from the theme, "A Voice for The Voice". The Lord has commissioned me to write this easy - read book entitled, *A VOICE FOR THE VOICE* for bishops, apostles, pastors, ministers, elders, deacons, missionaries and any one speaking on behalf of the Lord. While it is meant to inspire them in their role as voices, it also serves as a reminder that they are not the Voice, but rather they are voices for the Voice. This work gets its genesis from the biblical priest and prophet in the New Testament, namely

John the Baptist. The Lord has always used biblical figures in the Old Testament to speak on His behalf such as Abraham, Joseph, Moses, Joshua, Isaiah, Jeremiah, Amos, Esther, Haggai and Malachi to mention just a few. Malachi was the last voice to speak on behalf of the Lord in the Old Dispensation, the Old Covenant and the Old Testament. Thereafter, we had 400 or more years of silence, where no one heard a word from a prophet. After this period of silence, we had a voice that appeared on the scene. His name was John the Baptist. He was the child of Zechariah and Elizabeth. He was reported to have been the cousin to Jesus.

John the Baptist appeared in the oldest of the four gospels, the Gospel of Saint Mark, the first chapter. There was nothing royal looking about his attire. John Mark, in the writing of Saint Mark, was descriptive in telling us that John the Baptist's diet consisted of eating locusts and wild honey. John Mark is clear about depicting John the Baptist as a voice for the Lord Jesus Christ. He was to be known as a voice crying in the wilderness, as evidenced in Mark 1:3 which states, *"The voice of one crying in the wilderness, Prepare ye the way of the Lord, make his paths straight"*.

John the Baptist was very clear that he was a voice, but not "The Voice". He stated in Mark 1:8, "I indeed have baptized you with water: but he shall baptize you with the Holy Ghost". Consequently, this work helps to remind humanity of the *Caller*, who summons others to speak on His behalf. *A Voice for The Voice* is about affirming the called-out ones to stay focused on their divine assignment. The divine assignment is to be a voice for the Savior, and not for self. The Lord can use whom he pleases, including a donkey, to speak on His behalf. However, He has chosen men and women in particular to speak on His behalf. For those of you who are struggling to adhere to The Voice, may this work quicken your mind, heart and tongue, to submit your voice to The Voice. My desire and prayer is that this work will heighten the reader's sensitivity to be a truly committed and consistent voice, for the Lord.

A Voice *for* The VOICE

CHAPTER ONE
The Voice Is Always Calling Other Voices

The Voice that I'm speaking about in this book is the voice of the Lord. I understand there are all kinds of mundane, secular and demonic voices seeking to arrest the minds and spirits of people, whose intentions started out good, but later commenced to listening to a voice or voices other than the Voice of Jesus. In the midst of the Fall of Man in the book of Genesis, the Lord continues to select and appoint finite beings. The Lord in the past has always called people to serve as conduits, emissaries and ambassadors on His behalf. Speaking on behalf of the Lord usually is not a self-call or a man-made call, but it is a call that comes from Him. This is seen in John 15:16 which states, *"You have not chosen me, but I have chosen you, and ordained you, that ye should go and bring forth fruit, and that your fruit should remain: that whatsoever ye shall ask of the Father in my name, he may give it you"*. The Voice is a voice from above. The call from the Lord is irreversible and non-negotiable. Look at the call of Samuel who heard a voice but could not perceive it to be the Voice of the Lord. Enlightened by the priest Eli, Samuel was able to come to the realization that the Voice that kept coming to him was indeed The Voice of the Lord.

Let's briefly look at some other people He called, such as Isaiah and Jonah.

Isaiah was a man of means, very wealthy and an aristocrat. The Call of the Lord is never done in a vacuum. It so happened that one day Isaiah caught a glimpse of the glory of the Lord. This made him declare publicly that his hands were dirty, and he had been dwelling among people with unclean lips. The Lord then used one of his angels to touch his tongue as a sign that his sins had been forgiven. Thus, he could now become a mouth piece for the Lord and no longer for the demonic world. The Voice of the Lord extended *the called* to Isaiah, hence he stated in Isaiah 6:8, *"Also I heard the voice of the Lord, saying, Whom shall I send, and who will go for us? Then said I, Here am I; send me."*

Jonah, in his own case, was called to go and speak to the people in Nineveh. The call from the Lord always provides direction and content. Instead of yielding to the Voice of the Lord, he listened to himself and went the opposite direction of Nineveh, heading to Tarshish. At the end of the day, Jonah found himself praying for three days in the belly of a fish. Evidently, the Lord got his attention while in a powerless state and allowed the fish to release him. Jonah now did not waste any more time and headed to Nineveh, a place where the people were known to be stiff-necked. They objected Jonah in his attempt to tell them what the Lord had instructed him to share with them. Nevertheless, Jonah found himself back in the will of the Lord. Jonah knew it was better for him to be in Nineveh than to go in his own willful way. While in Nineveh, Jonah spoke on behalf of the Lord, however, his receptivity wasn't good at all. It was obvious that Jonah was called by the Lord to speak on His behalf even in a hostile environment. Jonah, no doubt, learned the valuable lessons of listening and acting on instructions given by God. The Lord can call whom He pleases to be a voice on His behalf. There are several families that have third and fourth generational Pastors who have been called by the Lord. The Lord has called rural Pastors, suburban Pastors and Urban Pastors. The Lord has called Pastors, in particular, around the world with and without theological education. The Lord has called Pastors who could hardly read or write their names. Many of them have been touched by the Lord. They have been given divine revelation knowledge along with special innate gifts from the Lord. As it related to Jesus, the question was raised in scripture, "What good can come out of Nazareth?" This question pointed to the home place of Jesus. I had this same question, in reference to my home town, asked of me. The question on more than one occasion has been raised, "What good can come out of Painter, Virginia?" This question was often asked after many colleagues viewed my accomplishments in the gospel ministry.

I am very clear about my call to ministry. I did not call myself, but the Lord called me. I was introduced to the Lord in my country church, New Mount Zion Baptist Church, in Painter, Virginia. It was fifty-five years ago that I was baptized in an outdoor pool on a cold winter morning. This church nurtured and spiritualized me in the formative years of my life. The Pastor of the church at that time was Pastor Willie A. Carter. He preached the gospel with fire and power. He preached from the scriptures and shared with the congregation the messages given to him by the Lord. He took me under his wings and began to develop me in ministry at an early age. At the age of 16, the Lord told me that, "One day I would be a voice speaking on His behalf".

Upon finishing high school, I attended Howard University. I recall praying to the Lord late one Sunday night in the month of November in 1973. In my prayer, I just thanked Him for how he had blessed me to come to Howard University. I thanked him for the blessing of a selfless sacrificing mother who loved the very ground her son walked on. In the midst of my prayer, the voice of the Lord spoke to me saying, "Commit yourself totally to me and go preach my word in a fragmented and dislocated world". I was not prepared, nor was I ready to step into the gospel ministry at the time. For two weeks I continuously heard the voice of the Lord; *commit yourself to my will and way.* After things began to go downhill, I can remember my surprise and dismay with a French test that resulted in an undesirable score that was a mystery to me. I truly felt that I had excelled on that exam. I knelt at the foot of my desk and told the Lord that you have my attention and I surrendered my life to Him. "Here I am, use me as you see fit".

On June 9, 1974, I was afforded the opportunity to preach my initial sermon at an afternoon service before a packed church at the New Mount Zion Baptist Church, Painter, Virginia. The title of that message was "Hitch Up to Move On". I dealt with the passage of scripture that pertained to the Rich Young Ruler who Jesus instructed to go sell all that he had. The sad commentary to that story was simply the Rich Young Ruler could not accommodate Jesus's request. *I was declaring* "Whatever I have, it belongs to the Lord; wherever you want me to go, I will go; whatever you want me to do, I will do it". When speaking before religious bodies, I like to start off with the song that says, "Hush, Somebody Is Calling My Name". Quite often I like to say, "hush, hush, hush, hush, the Lord is calling my name". Having been in ministry for forty-four years, thirty-seven years as a Pastor and two years as an International Presiding Bishop, the Lord has allowed me to fall down several times. But I can declare that every time He has come along and picked me up. I believe He has picked me to be a voice, not just to the church, but to other bishops, apostles, pastors, ministers, elders who are struggling with their fears, family, finances and future in ministry.

The Lord called imperfect men and women to speak on His behalf in biblical times. The Lord has called imperfect men and women to speak life and not death to a world soaking in sin. The Lord continues to use me, a broken and scared vessel, as a relevant voice for Him, in the global community.

CHAPTER TWO

Who Me? God Is Calling You to Be a Voice

The Voice serves to remind the called-out ones to always remember that, you have not called yourself, but the Lord has called you. Who me? This is a question that gets at the very fabric of humans representing the Lord. The Lord is perfect. As humans, we are imperfect. If one would put the righteousness of all who called on the name of the Lord together, it still would not be enough righteousness to have us dwelling with the Lord forever. It is because of the righteousness of the Lord that He allows one to stand and speak on His behalf. The Lord has no need for people who think more highly of themselves than they ought to. The Lord has no need of people who think they are doing Him a favor by consenting to be a voice for Him. The Lord has no need for the proud and the haughty.

God can use the "not sure" people. God can use those who will depend on His Voice as opposed to voices merely from sociological, psychological, or philosophical empirical data.

In my own walk with the Lord, I have had to be reminded to not devalue myself. I come from the country, single female head-of-household, limited resources but a whole lot of love. Older sisters, Maggie Helen and Clara Ann, stepped in to assist in the early socialization of my sister, Kerry, and I. My mother worked to care for her children. I had to ask myself the question, "Who Me?" At the age of thirteen, I was pulling weeds out of soy beans fields. I worked in the hot blistering sun during the summer months, ten hours a day earning seventy-five cents an hour and received a weekly pay of $37.50. At the age of fifteen, I worked at a produce factory grading white potatoes, cucumbers, tomatoes and string beans. The Lord spoke to me in the fields in Virginia and at the produce factory where I spent the majority of my time during the summer months. The Lord told me "These jobs are preparing you for a great work in my name".

As I looked back over my small beginnings, I now realized the Lord was preparing me to be a strong consistent voice for Him. He prepared me by way of an inquiring mind in the Sunday school. He prepared me by way of attending seminars and gaining spiritual education exposure through the Eastern Shore and Maryland Baptist Association. He prepared me through leadership trainings structured by the General Baptist Convention of Virginia. The Lord prepared me by enabling me to receive an undergraduate degree, with studies around collective behaviors of people, as well as the individual minds of those in the various group. The Lord prepared me through formalized theological study at Howard Divinity School. At the same time, he placed me at the historic Metropolitan Baptist Church, Washington, DC, working directly under the anointed and gifted pontificator, the Rev. Dr. H. Beecher Hicks, Jr. Dr. Hicks would remind persons like me that he was just another John the Baptist, a voice crying in the wilderness, prepare ye the way for the Lord today. The Lord was preparing me through the exposure of hearing from some of the greatest eloquent, analytical and insightful voices from the pulpit of the Metropolitan Baptist Church. Many of the other voices I heard are resting in the arms of the Lord. They were great voices always pointing to The Voice. Some of the names that readily come to mind have gone on to heaven such as the late Rev. Dr. William A. Jones, Rev. Dr. Harold A. Carter, Jr., Gardner C.

Taylor, Wyatt T. Walker, and Rev. Dr. Samuel Berry McKinney. The Lord called these voices for a season, to speak on His behalf. New seasons are on the horizon and the dawning of a new era is coming forth.

The Voice of the Lord is calling men and women from all over the world to be a voice of hope, faith, love to the global community. The perennial question remains, "Who, me?" I believe this question will always be asked by those who are aware of their limitations when called by the Lord to speak on His behalf. The perennial answer from the Lord will always be, "Yes, You".

CHAPTER THREE

A Voice as a Contemporary Priest/Pastor

The Priests or Pastors have been known to care for the congregation or parish. In the care of the flock, we are referring to such duties as preaching the gospel of good news, evangelism, praying and attending to the sick, burying the dead, counseling persons in crisis, administering the sacraments, performing marriage ceremonies, dedicating the babies and baptizing the unsaved. It is certain the list for the priest/pastor goes beyond the aforementioned duties.

The contemporary priest/pastor must be a voice for the Lord at all times. We live in a time where people would love to silence Christians all over the world. The priest/pastor is the main target. People no longer will tell the priest/pastor to shut up but rather accomplish the same in more sophisticated ways. The following are some of the ways the congregants are attempting to silence the pulpit:

- They stare at you when you are preaching as if to say you are "talking loud and saying nothing".
- They sit in the pews rendering negative feedback to anyone around them during the preaching hour.
- They text on their androids and iPhone during the preaching hour.
- They close their wallets and pocket-books during offering times.
- They blatantly turn their wrist on you to signal "You need to bring this sermon on in" while others continue to glance at the time.
- The church officers on the front row sleep during the preaching hour Sunday after Sunday.

Priests/Pastors are called to preach when things are going well in the church and when things are not going so well in the church. They should never allow congregants, money or status to deter them from preaching the gospel of the Lord Jesus Christ. I have always declared that I do not have a price tag on the gospel that I preach. In fact, the gospel I preach is not my gospel, it belongs to the Lord. I am assured that, as the Lord continues to take care of the birds and lilies of the field, He will surely take care of His own.

The attire for this office has been more civic in the past, meaning shirt and collar band or shirt and tie. Many of the younger pastors stand before their congregations or parishes with just a shirt with no tie and may sometimes wear a jacket. As a pastor, I am from the old school dress code for clergy. I personally feel that when you stand to speak on behalf of the Voice, you should dress in a clergy robe, civic attire or some specific manner to denote you are a clergy. During the time of John the Baptist, the gospel took special note to talk about his attire. Mark 1:6 says, *"And John was clothed with camel's hair, and with a girdle of a skin about his loins; and he did eat locusts and wild honey."*

Today, the old school priests and pastors are reminded that we are to take no thought of what we eat or drink. Just think about the great number of people who would have missed the message of repentance and baptism if they thought on these things. They would have missed the message about the Lord coming to baptize them with the Holy Ghost if they thought on these things. John the Baptist's attire was a distraction, but his voice still speaks loud and clear in this present age. We are called in this age to focus on the message, and not the attire.

The contemporary Priest/Pastor must be a voice of "Thus saith the Lord". The Priest/Pastor is expected to be many things to many people yet, they cannot be all things to all people. Thank God we are in an age of shared ministries with other ministers and lay leaders that also participate in the care, needs and concerns of a given congregation or parish.

The Priest or Pastor is called to be the mouth piece for the Lord at funerals. For the last thirty-eight years, I have been a voice speaking on behalf of the Lord to grieving families at a funeral home in Washington, DC. Many of the deceased were without a church home, but I am still called to be a light and to shine for the Lord. We have been called to shine for the Lord in dark places. Quite often, I remind them that our lives must be more than a hit, miss, or electric slide experience. Our shining for the Lord has to be more than carrying a big bible, wearing a cross or a tee shirt that says "Jesus loves me and I love him."

Our shining for the Lord must be about standing for Him at all cost. Our shining for Him must be about speaking good news from the bible and not bad news from some media outlet. Our shining for Him must be about feeding the hungry, clothing the naked and visiting those who are incarcerated. We are to always remind everyone that heaven is a prepared place for prepared people. As a voice for the Voice, I often recite the following gospel to grieving families: Saint John 14: 1-3 reads, *"Let not your heart be troubled: ye believe in God, believe also in me; in my Father's house are many mansions: if it were not so, I would have told you. I go to prepare a place for you; and if I go and prepare a place for you, I will come again, and receive you unto myself; that where I am, there ye may be also".* I often remind grieving families that this gospel may be old news, but it is still good news. It is yesterday's news, but it is still current news and it is still relevant news. This passage from the 14th chapter of Saint John took on a new meaning for me in the passing of my father and my mother. Grieving families do not need to hear our opinion or what we think. At the end of the day, they need to hear from The Voice of the Lord.

Priests and Pastors are called to share the Word of the Lord with those we encounter and in performing our various duties. The lesson for the congregants and the parish is not to focus on attire or time spent in worship, but to focus on the message from the priest or pastor.

A Voice *for* The VOICE

CHAPTER FOUR

A Voice as a Contemporary Prophet

Just as the Lord spoke to biblical prophets of yesterday such as Jeremiah, Daniel, Ezekiel, Joel, Amos, Hosea, and Micah, He is stilling speaking to prophets of today. The Voice of the prophet should always be about what the Lord has revealed. The prophets of old forewarned the Israelites of the destruction of the temple in Jerusalem, as well as the rebuilding of the temple in Jerusalem. Prophets, one after another, reminded the Israelites of their sinful ways and then called them to repentance.

As it was foretold by the prophet Joel in the book of Joel 2:28: "And it shall come to pass afterward, that I will pour out my spirit upon all flesh; and your sons and your daughters shall prophesy, your old men shall dream dreams, your young men shall have visions."

The prophecy of Joel is being actualized in this present age. Prophecy has not been given to males only, but to males and females. The Lord can use and will use whom He pleases when He so desires.

As a contemporary prophet, there are two prophets that have shaped my ministry; the biblical figure Amos and the late Dr. Martin Luther King, Jr. In the book of Amos, the prophet gave the biblical foundation for the called-out ones to be a voice for The Voice on behalf of the voiceless, powerless, downtrodden, and the disenfranchised. Amos 5: 21-24 says, *"I hate, I despise your feast days, and I will not smell in your solemn assemblies; though ye offer me burnt offerings and your meat offerings, I will not accept them: neither will I regard the peace offerings of your fat beasts; take thou away from me the noise of thy songs; for I will not hear the melody of thy viols; but let judgment run down as waters, and righteousness as a mighty stream".*

As prophets, we are called to speak when and wherever the monsters of injustice and inequality raise their heads. The late Reverend Dr. Martin Luther King, Jr. was a drum major for justice and fought inequality. He was a prophetic voice for The Voice. Some fifty years later, after the untimely death of Reverend Dr. King, his voice is still one most often quoted by people around the world, especially those who are being oppressed by their oppressors.

When I look back over my life as a Prophet, I cannot help but remember at the young age of twenty-seven, the Lord spoke to me to take a stand for unfairness and inequalities in Rhode Island. With this office of the Prophet, I assumed the advocacy posture of speaking on behalf of the oppressed. I was afforded the opportunity to serve as the President of the Ministerial Alliance of Rhode Island. The Ministerial Alliance was formed with a focus on advocacy for equality. The Ministerial Alliance challenged the Providence School System with what we perceived as their unfair hiring practices noted by empirical data from sources within the school system. My prophetic stance revolved around the hiring process and selection of administrators. While the preferred administrator endorsed by the Ministerial Alliance was not selected at that time, we were later instrumental in influencing the choice of a school principal.

I will never forget when the state of Rhode Island was considering whether or not to sanction the birthday of the late Dr. Martin Luther King, Jr. a legal state holiday. As the President of the Ministerial Alliance, I spoke at the hearing held at the State Capitol Building in Providence, Rhode Island. There was a gentleman who spoke before me and rallied against the legal state holiday. On three different occasions, he referred to the late Reverend Dr. King as communist in his speech. Something rose up in me and I could not allow him to continue to slander and belittle the late Reverend Dr. King any longer. Before I knew it, I had one foot on the desk in the state's chamber while yelling out, "I will not sit here and allow you call a man, who once fought for my rights, a communist, without giving us evidence. Needless to say, security surrounded me and the presider of the Hearing politely asked me to take a seat and indicated that we would take a five minute recess. He also directed the following comment to the former speaker: "Upon our return, if you do not have data to back up your claim, do not repeat it again in this hearing."

The Rhode Island Legislators approved the bill to make the birthday of the late Reverend Dr. Martin Luther King, Jr. a legal state holiday. I was the only non-legislator invited by the governor to witness the signing of that bill into law. As a prophet, I must say that was one of my most rewarding moments. Dr. King stated, "If you don't stand for something, you will fall for anything." I thank God for speaking through me and allowing me to stand for one who gave his life in hopes of establishing the beloved community.

There have been other experiences from Rhode Island to Maryland, where the office of prophet stood up in me. In Maryland, I connected with a clergy group to advocate against the Metro Board's plan to increase the cost of public transportation. I also joined other prophets in the fight to provide head start programs in socially deprived areas as well as other issues. Today, as the Lord speaks, my voice is available to be used.

A Voice *for* The VOICE

CHAPTER FIVE

A Voice as a Present-Day Servant

A Servant Leader is simply a Leader who has a mind to serve as the Lord directs. This kind of servant is more concerned about rendering service as opposed to finding a seat. This servant is not title conscious.

We live in an age where several pastors refer to themselves as Servant Leader. They have placed the Servant Leader title on their church stationery, websites, flyers as well as their social media pages. The gospel of Saint Mark depicts Jesus as a Servant Leader.

This type of servant has the heart and spirit of the Lord. This servant will be known for their deeds as opposed to words. The Lord went about doing good during His public ministry on earth. Jesus healed the sick, gave sight to the blind, fed the hungry, healed the crippled and lame, caused the deaf to hear, and cleansed lepers. Jesus did not pray to the Father to handle these situations, but He took care of them himself. Jesus did not seek approval from some board or leader to attend to spiritual matters of the church.

The biblical figure James says in James 2: 26, "For as the body without the spirit is dead, so faith without works is dead also."

The writer James reminds us in a clear and succinct way that, without work, our faith is dead on arrival. As I reflect over the last thirty-seven years of Pastoral Ministry, it has been one of providing services to the assigned congregation and the surrounding community. It has always been my spirit to develop an atmosphere whereby leaders and members would give more than lip service to the Lord. It has always been a part of my leadership style to lead by example. I have always been known to be a worker within the church. For me, it has never been a problem to pick up paper in a sanctuary or in a hallway. It has never been a problem to participate in cleaning projects inside and outside of a church. It has never been a problem to participate in the renovation projects of the church. It has never been a problem to assist missionaries in preparing sandwiches to feed the hungry or participate in packing school supplies to be shipped to Africa.

Servant leaders in this contemporary age are regarded as spiritual leaders walking in the footsteps of the Lord. People are not concerned about how well we dress or how well we speak. They are more concerned about our humility, as opposed to our holiness. There is a community proverb that states, "I rather see a sermon any day than to hear one".

Servant leaders are to be reminded that works speak louder than words, actions speak louder than inactivity; touch speaks louder than telling and reaching out speaks louder than failure.

My cry and prayer as a Servant Leader to the Lord, is the following: "Since you have blessed me, helped me, touched me, guided me and gifted me, let me hear your Voice even louder. Please let my voice be etched in deeds and not in creeds.

A Voice *for* The VOICE

CHAPTER SIX

Quotes from My Lips from The Voice

People often quote others from various perspectives and different fields of study. To name a few, this includes Albert Einstein, from the Mathematical world, Sigmund Freud from the Psychological world, Margaret Mead from the Anthropological world, John Dewey from the Educational world, Sir Isaac Newton from the Scientific world, John F. Kennedy from the Political world and Saint Augustine from the Religious world.

There is an African quote that says, "The success of one person is not predicated on that person but the total community".

Having been inspired over four decades by the Voice, I would like to share some of the thoughts by way of quotes that the Lord has spoken to me.

- Use what you Have! You will never be judged by the Lord on the basis of what you don't have but by what you do have.
- Love is not love until it goes down in the midst of the hurt only to love again.
- Faith is like being in a dark tunnel, but knowing there is light at the end of the tunnel.
- We are called to always walk by faith and never by sight.
- Great works can come by sight. Greater works come by Faith.
- You only pass this way but once so give your all to Jesus.
- We are beyond defeat.
- Rest always in the Lord.
- True Love can only be found in Jesus.
- After the rain in your life comes the sun in your life.
- Blessings are in the giving to others.

CHAPTER SEVEN

The Danger of Being a Voice

The praisers, affirmers, admirers, the Hosanna crowd can have one thinking more highly of one's self than one ought to. The biblical figure Paul, in speaking to the church at Rome, told them not to think more highly of themselves than they ought to. One can begin to believe everything people say about them in describing them as being a prolific and motivational speaker. This flattery can cause one to miss hearing and delivering the Savior's message. As a consequence, their voices have been reduced to echoes, whispers or tingling cymbals that make noise to advance themselves. The focus should be on advancing the kingdom of God. The congregants receive self-centered and entertaining messages. Spiritual Leaders must always be aware that our voices are temporal, but the Lord's Voice is eternal.

The self-promoting voice can never profess an intimate relationship with the Lord. Therefore, that person will never be able to be an authentic and compassionate voice for the Lord. The self-promoting voice will never find the peace and joy in serving the Lord. The danger of a self-promoting voice is one of ultimately being good for nothing. The Lord Jesus spoke on this matter in delivering the Sermon on the Mount, Saint Matthew 5:13 says,

"Ye are the salt of the earth: but if the salt has lost his savor, wherewith shall it be salted? It is thenceforth good for nothing, but to be cast out, and to be trodden under foot of men."

There is another danger of being a voice for the Voice. Many do not want to hear the voice for the Voice. In every congregation you will find the spirit of pointing Pharisees, fault-finding Sadducees, criticizing Scribes and negative elders. In the two traditional churches that I pastored, I encountered the Vocal Minority and the Silent Majority. The Vocal Minority expressed concerns loud about what they were displeased with. The majority of the congregants consist of the Silent Majority. They are affirming and praying for their church to press forward in doing kingdom works.

To be a voice for the Lord may look glamorous and easy. Below the surface, disappointment, disgust and even death can occur. Only one of the Lord's twelve disciples died a natural death. Stephen was stoned while John the Baptist and Paul were beheaded. The Lord was crucified on a Friday. The Lord rose from a tomb early on Sunday morning. The Lord did not just get up, but He declared all power is in His hands. Therefore, as spiritual leaders let us be reminded that after every crucifixion, there will be a resurrection.

A Voice *for* The VOICE

CHAPTER EIGHT

The Benefits of Being Obedient to The Voice

There is ONLY one Supreme, Sovereign, All-encompassing voice on earth, and that Voice is the Lord. The Lord spoke, and out of nothing, the earth began to take form and shape. His voice caused mountains to be created with enormous elevations. His voice caused mankind to have dominion, over living creatures below sea level and above sea level. His voice caused lions and tigers; bears and elephants to be submitted to mankind.

Being obedient to the Lord brings inexplicable internal satisfaction. The Lord calls, and when we answer, great rewards will come to us here on earth. However, the greater benefit is to be granted eternal citizenship in heaven. To know that you are in the will of the Lord causes the inner spirit to rejoice and to be glad.

I cannot count the number of times I visited members in the hospital to be a blessing to them, yet I received manifold blessings in return. My Consoling Voice at funerals has lifted people from despair to hope, from fear to faith, from tears to triumph and from weakness to strength. The benefits for me simply rest in the fact that the Lord allows me to be a blessing to others. As others are blessed, I believe I am doubly blessed.

Preaching the gospel has allowed me to see lives transformed before my eyes. Being a witness as others take on new leases in life within the congregation is very exciting and brings inner satisfaction. Being a witness to the testimony of former crack addicts testifying that they now reach for Christ instead of crack is very exciting and brings inner satisfaction. Transforming the lives of others because God used me as a vessel to deliver his word accents a fulfilled purpose driven life.

I am a strong believer and benefactor of the blessings from the Lord with long life, good health, sincere friends and a loving family. God has further blessed me to visit six of the seven continents. Like the Old Testament figure Joseph, I have been given the opportunity to speak from pits to palaces.

Every day when I open my eyes to see a new day, it is simply a blessing for me. Each time someone tells me how the Lord's message changed their thought patterns, aborted their path of destructions, removed them from the vices of the world or describe their new desire to live a life for the Lord, my soul gets happy over and over again. Today, I am blessed going and coming, largely because I said, "Yes to the Lord, use my voice as you want". The ultimate benefit for the global community today is the fact that the Voice is still calling and raising new voices to represent Him in the plan of restoring mankind.

Hush, hush, hush, the Voice is calling my name. The ultimate blessing for me today rests in the fact that the Lord is still calling my name to speak on His behalf.

A Voice *for* The VOICE

Conclusion

The Lord is the Voice. The Lord is counting on those whom He has called, to speak on His behalf. It is a privilege to be called-out to such an ardent task. Pastors and Spiritual Leaders have to be intentional about their self-care. Speaking on behalf of the Lord has the outward appearance of being glamorous and exciting, but this calling can be dangerous and harmful to your health, family and the global community.

To be the very best voice for the Lord, let me suggest the following:

- Stay connected to people who will constantly pray for you, as you embark on various speaking assignments.

- Read the bible regularly to continuously build, fortify, and restore the inner person.

- Always do a self-evaluation after every speaking assignment, for corrections, and/or celebrations.

- Establish a regular and consistent personal exercise program. The exercise program will increase your stamina and overall general health to enable you to be at your best physically when speaking for the Voice.

- Establish a Support Group of five to seven spiritual voices, to meet regularly to share counsel regarding personal and professional concerns, in an effort to reduce the stress of being a voice for the Lord.

Acknowledgements

It has been said it takes a village to raise a child. In the creation of this book, it has taken special people in the village to assist in *A Voice for the Voice*. Thanks to my wife, Eunice, for always reminding me about the need to share ministerial life experiences through a book. Special thanks to the spiritual illuminator, Rev. Henrietta C. Ekekezie, for taking me by the hand, and guiding me every step along the way. Thanks to the following persons who provided editorial and spiritual insights: Deacon Brenda Coley, Deacon Joyce Jenkins, Sister Geraline Boggs, Rev. Carlos Younger, Ambassador Marjorie Kornegay, and Bishop Eunice Turner.

Special thanks to the following:
Eli Blyden and the CrunchTime Graphics Team - Editorial expertise in the making of a successful book.

Special thanks to Maryellen O'Rourke and A & A Printing for the printing, and production of *A Voice for the Voice*.

Specials thanks to those spiritual leaders, who have prayed for the success of this book from India, Pakistan, Uganda, Kenya, Sierra Leone, Liberia, and the United States.

About the Author

Bishop Michael C. Turner, Sr.

**Bishop, Pastor, Author, Administrator,
Church Planter, Social Activist**

Bishop Michael C. Turner, Sr. is a native of Painter, Virginia. He was licensed to the Gospel Ministry at the New Mount Zion Baptist Church, Painter, Virginia (1974) by Reverend Dr. Willie A. Carter. He was ordained at the Metropolitan Baptist Church, Washington, D.C. (1980) by Reverend Dr. H. Beecher Hicks, Jr. He has been preaching the Gospel of Jesus Christ for 44 years. He is married to Bishop Eunice Thomas Turner.

Bishop Turner is an honor graduate of Howard University in Washington D.C., receiving the Bachelor of Arts Degree in Sociology and Psychology, 1977 (Cum Laude). He continued his training at the Howard Divinity School. In recognition of his consistent growth at the Divinity School, he was awarded the Daniel G. Hill award and graduated with a Master of Divinity in 1980. He continued his studies at the Boston University School of Theology in the area of

Church Administration. He received his Doctor of Ministry in the area of Church and Community, May 13, 1989 from Howard Divinity School.

He has toured Russia, Israel, Italy, Japan, Thailand, Korea, Hong Kong, Singapore, Canada, Caribbean, Mexico, Australia, New Zealand, Zambia, Soweto, Johannesburg, Uganda, Zimbabwe, Jamaica, Dominican Republic, South America, Nigeria and Liberia.

Bishop Turner serves as the Chaplain Writer for the newspaper, Prince Hall Masonic Digest. Bishop Turner served as a consultant in the writing of, *Tell The Story*, by James O. Stallings. He served as a past Editor of the official magazine for the Lott Carey Baptist Foreign Mission Convention.

He has given spiritual guidance in the establishment of First New Horizon Baptist Church of Clinton, Maryland; Miracle Center of Silver Spring, Maryland; Abundant Life Christian Ministries of Lanham, Maryland; Christ Vision Ministries, Worcester, Massachusetts; and Miracle Prayer Center of Khanewal, Pakistan. He serves as a Spiritual Leader to the following churches in Liberia: Sure Word Believer Chapel International, Mount Zion Christ Miracle Healing Ministries, Miracle Center of Faith Gospel Church, and Word of Power Ministry of Miracle Center. He was consecrated a bishop on March 5, 2016.

He is the founder and the Presiding Bishop of the International Evangelism College of Bishops established December 15, 2016.

He has served as Senior Pastor of The Miracle Center of Faith Missionary Baptist Church for the last 27 years.

A Voice *for* The VOICE

Follow Bishop Michael C. Turner Sr. on Social Media

Join Bishop Michael C. Turner's Facebook page to stay in touch:
www.Facebook.com/Michael Turner

Founder of the International Evangelism College of Bishops and the Organizer of The Miracle Center of Faith Missionary Baptist Church.

Twitter: @bishopturner55

Instagram: michaelturner0112

For more information please visit his website at:

Web: www.themiraclecenterfmbc.com

Email: bishopturner55@gmail.com

Phone: 1-301-350-2200

Mailing Address: 501 Hampton Park Boulevard, Capitol Heights, MD 20743

www.ingramcontent.com/pod-product-compliance
Lightning Source LLC
Chambersburg PA
CBHW071758040426
42446CB00012B/2611